PIRATES & SMUGGLERS

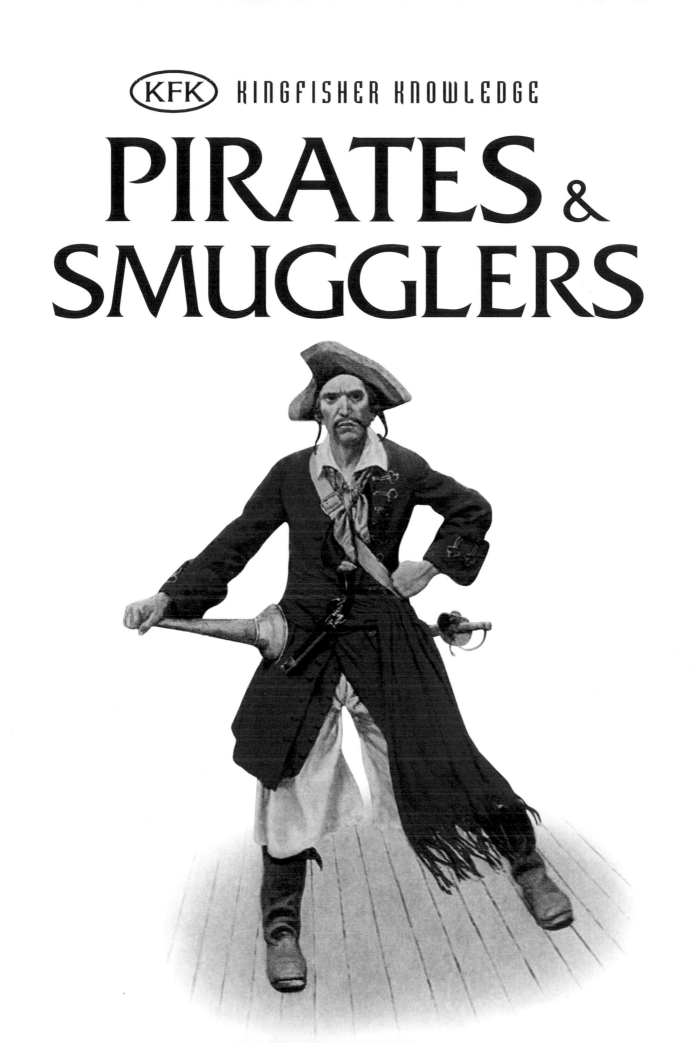

▼ A pirate attack was a truly bloodcurdling experience for sailors of the 17th and 18th centuries CE. In this painting by the American artist Frederick Judd Waugh (1861–1940), a vicious gang of buccaneers (see pages 20–21) rushes on board an enemy ship, heavily armed with pistols and razor-sharp cutlasses. Few crews put up a fight in the face of such a terrifying assault.

KFK KINGFISHER KNOWLEDGE

PIRATES & SMUGGLERS

Moira Butterfield

Foreword by
Captain Stephen Bligh

KINGFISHER

Editor: Russell Mclean
Designer: Carol Ann Davis
Consultant (illustrations):
  Gillian Hutchinson,
  National Maritime Museum
DTP manager: Nicky Studdart
Senior production controller:
  Lindsey Scott
Picture researcher: Rachael Swann
Indexer: Sue Lightfoot

KINGFISHER

Kingfisher Publications Plc
New Penderel House,
283–288 High Holborn,
London WC1V 7HZ
www.kingfisherpub.com

First published by Kingfisher Publications Plc 2005
10 9 8 7 6 5 4 3 2 1
1TR/0605/TWP/MA(MA)/130ENSOMA/F

ISBN-13: 978 0 7534 1102 5
ISBN-10: 0 7534 1102 4

A CIP catalogue record for this book
is available from the British Library.

Printed in Singapore

► Today's pirates use small, fast
boats to outmanoeuvre their prey.
These bandits are based in the Riau
Islands of Indonesia. Once they have
caught up with a target, the pirates
use a long bamboo pole with a hook
at the end to draw their own boat
alongside before boarding.

Contents

GO FURTHER...

INFORMATION PANEL KEY:

- websites and
  further reading

- career paths

- places to visit

NOTE TO READERS

The website addresses listed in this
book are correct at the time of publishing.
However, due to the ever-changing nature of the
internet, website addresses and content can change.
Websites can contain links that are unsuitable for children. The publisher
cannot be held responsible for changes in website addresses or content,
or for information obtained through third-party websites. We strongly
advise that internet searches should be supervised by an adult.

Foreword

Given my namesake, Captain William Bligh of *HMS Bounty* fame, some would say it was inevitable that one day I would become the Chief Executive of the Maritime and Coastguard Agency. Like William Bligh, I sailed as a ship's captain for more than 20 years. Unlike William Bligh, I never suffered a mutiny and, I am pleased to say, neither did I come into contact with pirates.

Whether it is Robert Louis Stevenson's character Long John Silver of 1881's *Treasure Island* or Captain Jack Sparrow in the Hollywood blockbuster *Pirates of the Caribbean*, we tend to associate pirates with not doing any real harm, living just beyond the rule of law, in search of treasure.

However, as you will see, the history of piracy and smuggling has had its fair share of scoundrels. From Captain Morgan and Blackbeard to the female pirates Anne Bonny and Mary Read, piracy has never been short of bloodcurdling characters, and you will no doubt enjoy reading about their adventures.

Films and novels have helped paint a picture of pirates as loveable rogues. But, in reality, piracy and smuggling was a cut-throat existence. Many innocent people lost their lives at the hands of pirates who would do anything for money, whether it was murder, theft or – in the case of the Napoleonic Wars – betraying the nation by selling secrets and housing French spies.

Smuggling is particularly important to the Maritime and Coastguard Agency because the original coastguard began as a response to smugglers who operated in the seas around Britain. In the 18th and 19th centuries CE, coastguards lived alongside smuggling every day – either trying to stop it or because the local community was connected with the trade.

Thankfully those terrifying days around the British coast have passed, but piracy remains a huge problem in other parts of the world, particularly in the South China seas and the Malacca Strait; parts of the Caribbean and South America; west and east Africa; and the Indian Ocean. Swashbuckling swords have been replaced by guns, as pirates target important shipping lanes. This modern activity threatens international trade, national economies and, most importantly, seafarers' lives.

Far from being harmless, modern pirates cause havoc and fear, and there is increasing evidence that piracy is linked to terrorism. Not only is the number of armed robberies at sea growing, but so is the threat of terrorists boarding and hijacking ships with the aim of attacking other ships and even the environment. Drug smuggling and terrorism are a far cry from searching for treasure on desert islands.

Piracy is as relevant today as it has always been. It is wonderful that this book outlines not only the rich history of piracy and smuggling, but also the modern-day threat that exists. I hope you will enjoy the read.

Captain Stephen Bligh
Chief Executive, Maritime and Coastguard Agency

CHAPTER 1

The first pirates

Think of a pirate and you probably imagine a flamboyant man wearing a frock coat, with a cutlass and perhaps a pegleg and an eyepatch. This image is based on pirates of the 18th century CE, but that is just one era in the long and violent history of piracy.

For thousands of years, people have sailed the oceans carrying valuable cargo to sell in different countries. Pirates have roamed the seas for just as long, attacking ships and coastal towns for profit.

The ancient Egyptians suffered attacks by 'sea peoples' as far back as the 13th century BCE. The ancient Greeks and Romans faced pirates too. And as sea trade grew in medieval times, so did the threat of ocean-going crime.

Mosaic showing the ancient Greek god Dionysus, in the form of a lion, driving pirates from his ship (see page 8)

Ancient times

From around 2500BCE onwards, great civilizations grew up around the Mediterranean. The sea was used more and more to transport goods such as grain and olive oil. Merchant ships sailed close to shore, because the sailors feared the open sea. They ran the risk of being ambushed by pirates, however, who lurked along the coast, ready to attack a passing vessel and steal its valuable cargo.

People stealers

In ancient times, the slave trade was big business. Mediterranean pirates could make a profit by snatching people from coastal settlements and selling them into slavery. Wealthy prisoners were sold back to their families for a large ransom. A story in Greek mythology tells of a pirate gang that captured Dionysus, the god of wine (see page 7). When Dionysus changed into a lion, the bandits jumped overboard in fright. As a punishment, the god turned the pirates into a school of dolphins.

▶ In the Mediterranean Sea, a pirate galley attacks a merchant ship carrying its valuable cargo of grain from Egypt to Rome. Cargo vessels were heavy, slow and powered by the wind alone. They were no match for the sleek, fast ships that the pirates used. To sink enemy vessels, galleys were armed with a battering ram. This was a wooden beam, strengthened with brass, that stuck out from the front of the ship.

Roman merchant ship

Most merchant vessels had small crews and few weapons

◀ As a young man, Julius Caesar (100–44BCE) was captured and held hostage by Cilician pirates. After his ransom was paid, Caesar was set free. In revenge, he hunted the pirates down and had them executed.

◀ This illustration from a Greek vase dates back to the mid-6th century BCE. It shows an example of the navy warships that the Greeks built to fight Mediterranean pirates.

Pirates prove useful

The seas around Greece are full of inlets and islands, which made ideal pirate hideouts. Piracy became a big problem for the Ancient Greeks, who built fleets of warships to fight back. Sometimes the Greek city-states went to war with each other, however, and then the Greek leaders encouraged pirates to attack enemy ships. This is an early example of rulers deliberately using pirates to harm their enemies.

Romans versus pirates

As the Roman Empire grew in power, it set out to crush the pirates of the Mediterranean. First, they were driven eastwards. By the 1st century BCE, Cilicia, an area of what is now Turkey, had become the centre of piracy. The bandits threatened Rome's vital grain supply from Egypt, so in 67 BCE the famous soldier Pompey the Great (106–48 BCE) attacked their bases from sea and land, wiping out the pirates.

Pirate galley

Once the boats were locked together, well-armed pirates would swarm onto the cargo ship

◀ Galleys were used by both pirates and navies in ancient times. The basic design was Greek in origin, and was copied by the Romans. The galleys carried a sail, but they were mainly powered by two or three banks of oarsmen. This made them fast and easy to manoeuvre alongside a cargo vessel.

Wooden fighting turret

Some pirate galleys had eyes painted on the prow (front) as a good-luck charm, and to make the ship look more impressive

Oarsmen inside the galley provided ramming power

▼ A fleet of Viking warships, or longboats, speeds towards the coast of northeastern England, ready to raid a Christian church for its metal treasures. The earliest recorded Viking attack in England was on the monastery of Lindisfarne Island in CE793. When they raided, the Vikings also grabbed people to ransom or sell as slaves.

Longboats had a shallow draught (depth), making them easy to land on a beach or row up a river

Powerful oarsmen, ready to join the attack

Steering oar

The northern menace

From the 5th century CE, the Roman Empire crumbled and for the next few hundred years piracy spread once more. In northern Europe, barbarians raided ships and coastal settlements mercilessly, striking fear into ordinary people with their lightning attacks and violence.

Overlapping wooden planks, hammered together with iron nails, made the longboats strong enough to sail the open seas

Viking raiders

The Vikings of Scandinavia were the most feared of the northern raiders. From the 8th to the 11th centuries CE, they menaced the coasts of northern Europe. The Vikings were expert sailors who could travel far across the open sea and then sail up rivers, taking towns and villages by surprise. Before the inhabitants could hide their valuables, fierce warriors would swarm ashore to kill and steal.

The Vikings measured their wealth by the amount of precious metal they owned. They liked to raid Christian monasteries and churches because of the metal treasure they would often find. The Vikings stole great quantities of it, much of which was melted down to be made into jewellery or metal bars. Sometimes they simply cut up treasure into pieces, to use as money.

The pirate monk

England and France were often at war during the Middle Ages, and both nations could turn a blind eye to piracy when it hurt the enemy. One pirate was a former priest, Eustace the Monk (c.1170–1217). Under the protection of King John of England (ruled 1199–1216), he raided French ships in the English Channel. Then he swapped sides and was paid by the French to attack England. He was captured by the English, and beheaded on board his own ship.

Baltic barbarians

The Baltic Sea was an area of great trading importance in the 14th century CE. Many large ports joined together to create a trading group called the Hanseatic League, and their well-laden ships became pirate targets. One of the most famous bandits was Klaus Störtebeker. He terrorized the Baltic during the 1390s, but was finally captured by a Hanseatic fleet in 1402. The pirate and 70 of his followers were taken to Hamburg, in Germany, and executed.

▲ The name of the Baltic pirate Störtebeker (died 1402) means 'down in one gulp'. To join his crew, a sailor had to pass an unusual test – to drink an enormous beaker of beer in one swallow.

Slave pirates

In the 15th and 16th centuries CE, North Africa was ruled by the Turkish Ottoman Empire. Muslim pirates called corsairs set sail from ports along the Mediterranean coast to attack Christian trading ships and settlements. The corsairs were after valuable goods – Christians to sell as slaves. Over a period of 200 years, up to a million Europeans are thought to have been kidnapped and enslaved. The corsairs were called barbarians by their Christian enemies, or Barbary pirates for short.

▲ Corsair leaders such as the Barbarossa brothers became fabulously wealthy, with their own palaces and powerful galley fleets. This painting shows Khayr ad-Din (c.1470–1546), the younger of the two brothers. As young men, they were given the nickname Barbarossa because it described their red beards.

The pirate coast

The North African cities of Algiers, Tunis and Tripoli were the corsair strongholds, and also the location of the slave markets that the pirates supplied. Famous corsair captains included the Barbarossa brothers and Murat Rais (c.1535–1638), who sailed as far as Ireland to raid coastal villages, kidnapping everyone and leaving whole areas deserted. But not all the corsairs were Arabs. Some Christian sailors 'turned Turk' and joined in the lucrative slave-snatching.

Corsair galleys

The corsairs used sleek, fast galleys with oars and triangular sails to outmanoeuvre their prey. The oars were pulled by naked slaves, bullied and whipped into rowing faster by Muslim soldiers called Janissaries. The front of a galley was armed with a cannon, so it could fire forwards at the enemy while presenting a very narrow target for return fire. Once a galley had caught up with the enemy, the armed Janissaries would swarm on board for a hand-to-hand battle.

◀ Christian priests (shown here on the left) often tried to buy back slaves from the corsairs, who sold them at slave markets on the Barbary coast.

Slaves for sale

Muslim corsairs sold their captives in the thriving slave markets of the North African coast or forced them to row in their galleys. The life of a galley slave was short and brutal, so new ones were always needed. Female captives were usually sold into harems. At one time, there were said to be so many Christian slaves in Algiers that you could buy one for an onion.

▼ This painting, from CE1670, shows a fleet of Dutch merchant ships being attacked by Barbary corsairs. One of the corsair galleys is in the foreground. Corsairs on the bow (front) and stern (rear) aim arrows at a Dutch vessel. Galleys were sleek and fast, capable of sudden bursts of high speed for as long as the slave oarsmen could last the pace.

Pirate knights

Muslim corsairs and merchant ships were regularly attacked by Christian sailors led by the Knights of St John – a brotherhood set up to fight the corsairs' religion of Islam. At first the knights were backed by Christian rulers, but eventually they turned to piracy. The Muslim slaves who rowed their galleys were treated just as brutally as the Christians who suffered at the hands of the Barbary pirates.

Plundering privateers

In the 16th century CE, European nations competed to conquer new lands and bring back profitable cargoes. At the forefront of exploration was Spain, with valuable colonies in the Caribbean, Central America and South America. Spain was a powerful Catholic country, and its Protestant enemies tried to disrupt Spanish trade by hiring private sea captains to attack on their behalf. These licensed pirates were called privateers.

▼ Sir John Hawkins (1532–95) was a hero to the English because he raided Spanish ships and fought the Armada in 1588. But to others he was a criminal who started the slave trade between Africa and America by illegally selling west African slaves to the Spanish colonies.

Letters of marque

European rulers issued letters of marque – formal contracts by which the monarch would hire a privately owned ship and its crew, and send it to disrupt enemy sea trade. A letter of marque authorized acts of piracy, and ensured that the monarch took a share of any cargo that was seized. It was a cheap way to wage war and make a large profit at the same time.

Built for speed

Privateer ships were sleeker and faster than the sturdy Spanish treasure ships, or galleons (see pages 16–17). They used cannon to batter a galleon into submission, avoiding the risk of a hand-to-hand fight on board.

Privateer heroes

European rulers rewarded privateers well. Francis Drake (1540–96) was knighted by Queen Elizabeth I (ruled 1558–1603) for attacking Spanish ships in the 1570s. In 1588, a large Spanish fleet called the Armada set sail to invade England. Privateers such as Drake and John Hawkins helped to defeat the fleet and became national heroes. More than a century later, René Duguay-Trouin was honoured by the French king, Louis XIV, for his attacks against the English.

Privateers turn pirates

The sea-going nations of Europe were not always at war during the 16th century. But even though the privateers were only licensed to act in wartime, this did not stop them attacking ships in times of peace. The lure of big profits was simply too great. Queen Elizabeth I would often turn a blind eye to the peacetime activities of her privateers, whom she called 'sea dogs'. Privately, she even supported their attacks, which brought her great wealth.

▼ Privateers helped to defeat the Spanish Armada. They used their seamanship and knowledge of the English coast to outsmart the enemy, although the weather also helped them.

▶ French privateers were called corsairs. René Duguay-Trouin (1673–1736), the most well-known corsair, captured 16 warships and around 300 merchant vessels during his 23-year career.

◄ These Spanish coins came from the wreck of a pirate ship called the *Whydah* (see page 58). Perhaps they were stolen from a Spanish treasure galleon.

BAHAMAS

GULF OF MEXICO

Havana

CUBA

Santiago de Cuba

The Spanish Main

The area known as the Spanish Main included the Spanish colonies of the Caribbean, Central America and the northern shores of South America. The wealth of the Spanish Main became legendary, and the galleons that carried the treasure back to Spain were the number one target for privateers during the 16th century CE.

JAMAICA

Port Royal

Belize

Lands of treasure

In the 1520s and 1530s, Spanish conquerors, known as conquistadors, brutally overthrew the Aztec and Inca nations of Central and South America. The Spanish ruthlessly stole the locals' wealth and discovered great reserves of precious metals. Using slaves from both the local area and west Africa, they mined huge quantities of silver, which they sent back to Spain by sea.

CENTRAL AMERICA

The journey home

Individual ships were vulnerable to attack, so the Spanish sought safety in large numbers. Once a year, an enormous fleet of up to 100 ships would set out to transport the treasure home. Although sturdy and well defended, the Spanish galleons were often slow and difficult to sail. Eagle-eyed privateers cruised the Main on the lookout for unprotected treasure ships that had been separated from the fleet by darkness or bad weather.

Cartagena

Portobelo

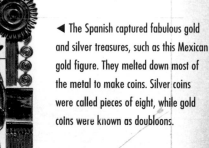

◄ The Spanish captured fabulous gold and silver treasures, such as this Mexican gold figure. They melted down most of the metal to make coins. Silver coins were called pieces of eight, while gold coins were known as doubloons.

► This painting shows pirates in a small boat about to board a slow, heavily laden treasure galleon in the Caribbean.

Tortuga

HISPANIOLA

● **Santo Domingo**

Isla Vaca (Cow Island)

Lumbering galleons

Galleons sailed well with the wind blowing from behind but were much slower against the wind, when they were most easily caught by privateers. Once a galleon had been chased down, a privateer would use cannon fire to try and force a surrender. If hand-to-hand fighting broke out, the Spanish stood a better chance because they were well armed with muskets, rapiers and knives.

Deadly pirate hunter

In the 1540s and 1550s, Spanish galleons were attacked by French pirates based in what is now Florida, USA. Spanish nobleman Pedro de Menendez de Avilles (1519–74) was sent to hunt them down. In 1565, he seized the pirates' base at Fort Caroline while they were at sea. The inhabitants were slaughtered, and the pirates executed when the Spaniard caught up with them.

▼ The Spanish Main was a vast geographical area centred around the many islands of the Caribbean, such as Cuba and Hispaniola. This 16th-century map shows some of the major ports in the region.

Maracaibo

SOUTH AMERICA

TRINIDAD

SUMMARY OF CHAPTER 1: THE FIRST PIRATES

The Vikings ransacked Christian churches because they were often full of valuable treasures, such as this book with a jewelled cover.

Pirates prey on people

Pirates have brought terror to the oceans since sea-going trade began. For thousands of years they have preyed on ships carrying valuable cargo, and attacked coastal towns and villages.

From ancient times, pirates were engaged in seizing people. Ancient Greeks, Romans, Vikings, Barbary corsairs and European privateers all made money from capturing and selling people as slaves, sometimes snatching them from their own homes as well as from ships. Rich captives were ransomed back to families who could afford to rescue them, but poor people were sold on for a high profit.

Rulers and pirates

From early times, kings and queens have used pirates for their own ends, supporting them by lending them ships, giving them permission to attack enemies, and often taking a share of the profits from their raids. In the 16th century CE, the link between rulers and pirates was particularly strong. European countries went to war for religious reasons, and also to stop each other trading overseas and colonizing new lands. Monarchs such as England's Queen Elizabeth I encouraged pirates by handing out privateer licenses.

The Spanish Main

Central America, northern South America and the islands of the Caribbean – the Spanish Main – were a hotbed of pirate activity during the 16th century. England and France sent privateers to the region to attack Spanish galleons, which were loaded with gold and silver treasures. The privateers became heroes in their own countries, but to others they were seen as ruthless and violent criminals.

Go further...

To find out more about ships and pirates through the ages, visit the website of the National Maritime Museum at Greenwich, in London: www.nmm.ac.uk

Read about the reconstruction of a Viking longship on the website of the Roskilde Viking Ship Museum: www.vikingeskibsmuseet.dk

The World of Pirates by Philip Steele (Kingfisher, 2004)

Life in Ancient Rome by Simon Adams (Kingfisher Knowledge, 2005)

For younger readers:
The Kingfisher Treasury of Pirate Stories (Kingfisher, 2004)

Archaeologist
Studies the past by working on historical sites to reveal old ruins and objects without damaging them.

Archivist
Conserves and catalogues historical documents.

Conservator
A highly trained technician who is a specialist in preserving historical objects, perhaps using special tools and chemicals.

Curator
In charge of a museum area, ensuring the exhibits are kept in an environment that will keep them safe and in good condition.

Visit Rome, the capital of Italy, where you can see ancient ruins and museums dedicated to Roman life. The port area of ancient Rome was called Ostia.

Take a trip back in time to a Viking town at the Jorvik Viking Centre:
Coppergate, York YO1 9WT, UK
Telephone: +44 (0) 1904 643211
www.jorvik-viking-centre.co.uk

Visit the reconstruction of Francis Drake's ship, the *Golden Hind* (exhibition open from March to October):
The Quay, Brixham TQ5 8AW, UK
Telephone: +44 (0) 1803 856223
www.goldenhind.co.uk

A scene from a Hollywood film, *Blackbeard the Pirate*, set at the time of the Golden Age

CHAPTER 2

The Golden Age

A fast, sleek pirate sloop glides out of the mist and up behind a lumbering merchant ship weighed down with precious cargo. A murderous pirate crew swarms aboard, led by a crazy captain.

This is a scene familiar from movies, but also from eyewitness accounts written during the 'Golden Age' of piracy – roughly between CE1690 and 1730 – when crime was at its height off the American coast and in the Indian Ocean. Writings of the time tell of extraordinary pirate characters such as the fearsome Blackbeard and the wily Captain Morgan. These villains became celebrities whose adventures scandalized and fascinated readers in Europe. Since then, their true-life escapades have been mixed with the imagination of writers to create the ever-popular image of the pirate.

Buccaneers

The Golden Age of piracy began with a ragged group of lawless hunters. For years the Spanish had tried to keep other countries away from the Caribbean, but in the early 17th century CE a group of French former sailors settled on the island of Hispaniola. They lived off the land, hunting wild cattle and preserving the meat in huts called smokehouses, or boucans. They became known as boucaniers, or buccaneers. When Spain tried to drive the hunters out, they turned to a life of piracy, attacking Spanish ships and coastal settlements.

▲ Buccaneers were notoriously cruel, especially Frenchman François l'Ollonais (1635–c.1669). He was said to have ripped out the heart of a prisoner and stuffed it into another captive's mouth.

▼ Henry Morgan was a Welsh sea captain who became a buccaneer. His privateer's licence meant he had to pay the English monarch a share of any prizes he captured at sea. To get round this rule, he often attacked coastal towns. Here, Morgan and his men loot the town of Portobelo, Panama, in 1668. They are trying to find out from a prisoner where treasure might be hidden.

Pirate island

When the buccaneers were driven out of Hispaniola (present-day Haiti and the Dominican Republic), they settled on the nearby island of Tortuga (see map on page 17). Despite Spanish attempts to smash the hideout, the number of buccaneers grew as the island attracted runaway slaves, French pirates and fortune seekers.

Legends are born

Tortuga became one of the most infamous pirate bases in the Caribbean. It was run as a kind of pirate republic, led by daring and vicious captains. We know a lot about them thanks to a book called *Bucaniers of America*, written by a pirate surgeon, Alexandre Exquemelin (1645–1707). He told of treasure raids, terrible cruelties and lucky escapes. He explained how the buccaneers would return to Tortuga with their booty, to party and plan more raids. His book was a bestseller in the 17th century, and it is the basis for many of our modern ideas about pirates.

The Welsh buccaneer

The English government of the time used pirates as an unofficial navy, to capture land. It gave a privateer's licence to Henry Morgan (c.1635–88), one of the most famous buccaneers. His raids on Spanish settlements during the 1660s netted him a fortune. He was knighted by the British, and eventually became governor of Jamaica in 1674.

Morgan's exploding ship

Henry Morgan had a fleet of ships, on loan from the British. One night he held a meeting of his captains on board a warship called the *Oxford*. As the officers sat round the table, a stray spark – perhaps from a musket being fired for fun, or a pig-roast – ignited a barrel of gunpowder. It blew up and killed 350 men. Miraculously, Morgan escaped. The scattered wreck of the *Oxford* was located by divers in 2004, off the coast of Haiti.

▼ The original French hunters used a cutlass to butcher the animals they caught on Hispaniola. It became a favourite pirate weapon because it was short and easy to carry. This illustration of a cutlass fight dates from 1685.

Blackbeard's time

As Europe became more peaceful in the late 17th and early 18th centuries CE, the privateers of the Caribbean and American Atlantic coast lost their official backing – but they carried on being pirates because it was so profitable. Some, such as the notorious Blackbeard, continued to raid cargo ships in the Caribbean. Others preyed on slave vessels along the west coast of Africa or sailed into the Indian Ocean to raid ships on trading routes from India and the Far East. The trip from America to the Indian Ocean via Africa and back was known as the pirate round.

▶ The pirate round took ships from North America across the Atlantic to prey on slave ships off the Guinea coast of west Africa. Then they sailed round the Cape of Good Hope to raid vessels in the Indian Ocean, before heading home.

▼ Edward Low (died 1724) was one of the cruellest pirates of Blackbeard's time. Legend says that he once cut off and cooked a man's lips. Here, one of Low's equally vicious crew members shoots a prisoner at point-blank range.

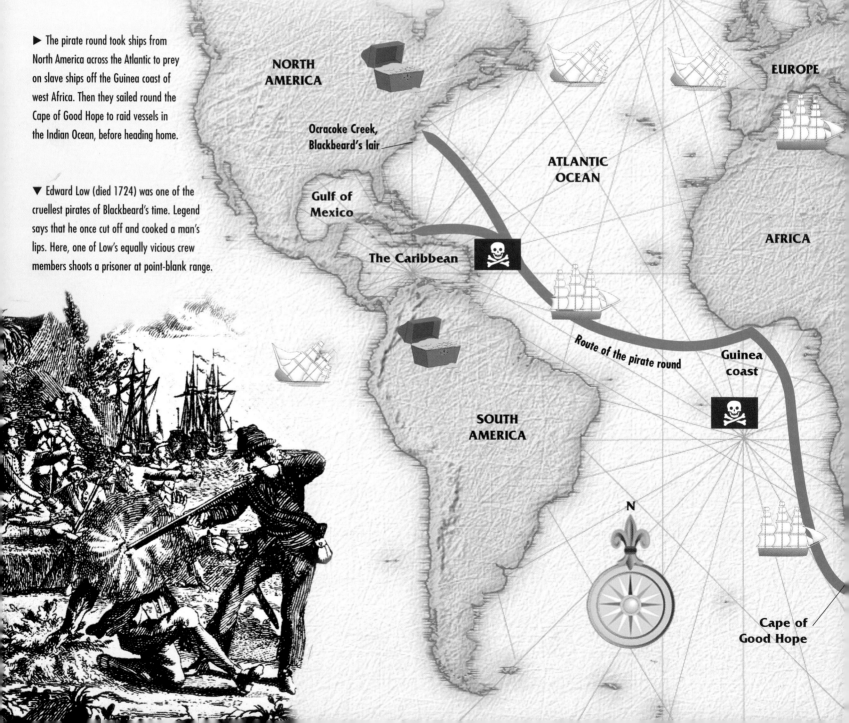

NORTH AMERICA

Ocracoke Creek, Blackbeard's lair

Gulf of Mexico

The Caribbean

ATLANTIC OCEAN

EUROPE

AFRICA

Route of the pirate round

Guinea coast

SOUTH AMERICA

N

Cape of Good Hope

Ships of the Golden Age

For long ocean voyages, the pirates of the Golden Age preferred three-masted, square-sailed ships, usually vessels they had captured. For shallow inshore waters, small sloops were ideal. These were fast and manoeuvrable, with triangular sails attached to a bowsprit – a long wooden beam at the front of the ship. When a prize was sighted, the pirates would come up astern (from behind) to avoid the enemy's main cannon, which usually pointed sideways.

The infamous Blackbeard

Blackbeard (died 1718) is the most famous pirate of this era, although he operated for only two years. He was English, and his real name was probably Edward Teach. He cruised the Caribbean and the Gulf of Mexico in a captured French slave ship, seizing prizes and taking them to a hideout in Ocracoke Creek, off the coast of North Carolina, North America. Here, Blackbeard bribed the authorities to turn a blind eye to his activities and sold his booty to the locals.

Death of a legend

Blackbeard felt safe in the shallow waters of his Ocracoke lair. But late in 1718, the British governor of Virginia, fearing growing lawlessness, sent a Royal Navy expedition to find him. Led by Lieutenant Robert Maynard, the British took the pirate fleet by surprise, and in the bloody fight that followed, Blackbeard was killed. His head was hung from the bowsprit of Maynard's sloop (see page 32). Members of the legendary pirate's crew were captured and hanged.

▼ Blackbeard terrified his enemies. When he went into battle, burning fuses in his hair created a cloud of choking black smoke. He and his crew were often drunk on a cocktail of rum mixed with gunpowder, and it was even said that he killed members of his crew from time to time, just to show who was in charge.

ASIA

INDIAN OCEAN

Madagascar

KEY

Pirate hotspot

Pirate attack

Nothing struck fear into the heart of a sailor as much as the sight of a group of desperate pirates, armed to the teeth, climbing over the side of his ship. Pirate captains had to employ a range of strategies to capture a prize successfully. They used stealth, deception, threats of violence and, ultimately, overwhelming force to get their prey to surrender.

Bloody battles

During the late 17th and early 18th centuries CE, life at sea was particularly dangerous for all sailors, both pirates and law-abiding seamen. Conditions were harsh, the sea was a dangerous place and life expectancy was short. Pirates were notorious for showing no mercy to those who fought against them. Hand-to-hand battles were brutal and bloody, and many men on both sides could be killed in action.

Boarding tactics

Pirates preferred to frighten a prize into surrender, but if they had to board they threw grappling irons – metal hooks on the end of a long rope – into the rigging of a treasure ship to draw it close to the pirate vessel. Tar grenades might be thrown to cause confusion – either by setting fire to rigging and sails or by creating thick smoke. Most seamen went around barefoot, so spiked metal weapons called caltrops were thrown on deck to wound the treasure ship's defenders. Once the pirates had set foot on board, they attacked with cutlasses, pistols, muskets, axes and daggers.

▲ Having softened up the enemy, pirates swarm up the steep wooden sides of a Spanish galleon to overwhelm the defending crew. Armed with swords and guns, the pirates are prepared to risk death for a rich prize.

◀ Movie pirates, such as Captain Jack Sparrow in *Pirates of the Caribbean*, usually wear lots of jewels. This is, in fact, true to history. Pirates of the Golden Age often dressed in fine clothes and jewellery stolen from wealthy captives. They liked to look like rich aristocrats as a way of parading their success.

▶ This action-packed scene shows the battle that killed Blackbeard (see page 23) in 1718. Cannon and gunfire added to the havoc during the fight. A cannonball smashing into a ship's deck could send deadly wooden shards flying everywhere, while swivel guns mounted on pivots could spray an enemy deck with gunshot.

Piracy or death

The defeated crew members were offered a choice – they could join the pirates, or die. Not surprisingly, many turned to piracy. In some ways, a pirate's life was better than an ordinary seaman's. Pirates had more freedom from authority, the chance to make lots of money, and the prospect of drunken parties on a Caribbean island. When a naval officer was caught, the pirates soon found out how he had treated his men. If he had been cruel, he was given a taste of his own medicine.

Jolly Roger

The Jolly Roger, the skull-and-crossbones flag flying from the topmast of a ship, is the most well-known pirate symbol of all. Pirate flags were flown to warn ships that the bandits would kill anyone who opposed them. The name is thought to come from the French 'jolie rouge' ('pretty red one'), because pirate flags were originally blood-red.

▲ Each pirate captain had his own flag, often decorated with symbols of death. Blackbeard's flag shows a skeleton holding an hourglass and pointing an arrow at a bleeding heart. The message was clear: 'You don't have much time – surrender or die!'

Life on board

The thrill of chasing a prize did not come every day for pirates of the Golden Age. In between short bursts of fighting, pirates had to put up with long periods of boredom, exhausting chores to keep the ship in good condition, and terrible food. Even when there were no battles to be fought, a pirate's life was very dangerous, with a high risk of death by accident or disease.

▲ The many sails of a large 18th-century ship had to be kept in good condition at all times. Most crews had a sailmaker who could repair ripped sails with a large needle. At sea, the sails could often be adjusted from the deck, but sometimes seamen had to scramble up the rigging (ropes) to tie the canvas sails to the wooden poles.

Food and drink

Hard tack biscuits, made of flour and water, made up the largest part of many sailors' diets. On board, the biscuits soon became infested with weevils. Before eating them, sailors would tap the biscuits to knock the weevils out. Sometimes, hens were kept on the ship, and the crew would also catch fish and turtles to eat. To drink, there were barrels of water and beer. Sailors often used alcohol to hide the bad taste of stale water.

Sores from scurvy

Fresh food quickly went rotten on board ship, so most food had to be preserved by either smoking or salting. On long voyages, many sailors suffered from a disease called scurvy, which is caused by a lack of fruit and vegetables. It left their teeth rotten and their skin covered in sores. In 1753, it was discovered that eating citrus fruit, such as limes and lemons, could prevent the disease.

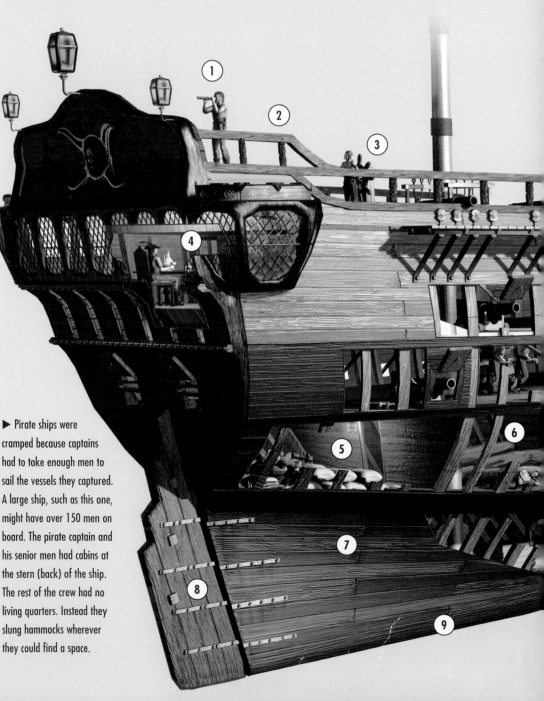

▶ Pirate ships were cramped because captains had to take enough men to sail the vessels they captured. A large ship, such as this one, might have over 150 men on board. The pirate captain and his senior men had cabins at the stern (back) of the ship. The rest of the crew had no living quarters. Instead they slung hammocks wherever they could find a space.

Surgery at sea

Ships of the Golden Age were so dirty that even minor illnesses or wounds could be life-threatening. Most crews included a ship's surgeon, who often had no medical training at all. The usual treatment for an injured limb was to cut it off, with no painkiller except alcohol, which the patient drank to dull the pain. Because there were no antiseptics, the chances of dying from an infection after surgery were high.

The pirate code

Surprisingly for such cut-throat gangs, some pirate crews drew up strict codes of behaviour to avoid fighting between the men. Often, women and gambling were banned from the ship. Some of the measures were very advanced for their day. For example, crew members could vote on important matters. They also had the right to an equal share of stolen loot, and pirates who were wounded in action often received financial help.

▲ In the navy, one of the harshest punishments was to be flogged (whipped) with a cat o' nine tails — a whip with nine knotted tails. Victims were scarred for life, or even died. Many pirates were former navy sailors who bore grudges against their old officers. Some probably carried the scars of naval floggings. No wonder pirates often renamed their captured ships The Revenge.

KEY

1. Sailor on watch
2. Poop deck
3. Helmsman steering the ship
4. Captain's cabin
5. Food stores
6. Sail store
7. Hull
8. Rudder
9. Keel
10. Cannon
11. Mainmast
12. Rowing boat
13. Oarsmen
14. Cannonball store
15. Water and beer barrels
16. Flogging on the forecastle
17. Anchor
18. Bowsprit

◀ A sailing ship's oars were used when there was no wind, or when the ship was entering a port.

▶ Rats were unwelcome passengers on all types of ship at this time. They could cause great damage by eating food stores and damaging equipment. They also carried serious diseases. On a long voyage the rats would breed, and thousands could end up on board, fouling the stores and gnawing the ropes and wood.

Pirates on land

Pirates did not spend all their time at sea, and they looked forward to a riotous time on land as a reward for the hardships of life on the waves. Captains searched for a safe haven that could be fortified against attack from the authorities, and where their crew could spend money. In the Indian Ocean, sparsely populated Madagascar was perfect, while the Caribbean was dotted with notorious pirate haunts, such as Port Royal in Jamaica and the island of Tortuga.

▲ Because life at sea was often brutal and short, many pirates felt that saving for a comfortable retirement was a waste of time. They spent their money ashore, often gambling it away. This pack of 19th-century playing cards was confiscated from a captured pirate ship by a British naval officer.

Wildness on shore

Once pirates set foot on the shore, they looked for release from the boredom and dangers of life at sea. They had plenty of money to lavish on drinking, gambling and entertaining women. Many pirates gained wealth beyond the dreams of an ordinary sailor, but they also managed to fritter it away. Sometimes they would spend the equivalent, in today's money, of thousands of pounds in a single night. Drunkenness was widespread, with local Caribbean rum being the favourite drink.

The dream of Libertatia

A lot of information about pirates comes from Charles Johnson's book, *The History of Pyrates*, published in 1724. It mentions Captain Misson, who set up a pirate republic called Libertatia on the island of Madagascar. It was said to be democratic – all pirates were equal, and any loot was shared. Many historians dismiss Libertatia as a myth, but it is true that some pirates settled on Madagascar, and that the pirate code was democratic.

Buried treasure

Perhaps the greatest pirate myth is that hoards of captured treasure were buried on remote islands, ready to be tracked down later with a coded treasure map. There are many legends of hidden loot and rumours of pirate gold, but very little has turned up – so it is possible that these tales have been exaggerated by storytellers.

Kidd's booty

One of the most famous treasure tales relates to Captain William Kidd (see page 33). He was licensed by the British authorities to hunt French pirates in the Indian Ocean. However, he also attacked British ships to boost his profits. He sailed to the east coast of America and is said to have buried a fabulous treasure on Long Island, east of New York. As yet, no-one knows the truth about Kidd's booty, although many have searched for it.

▲ The flag of Captain Bartholomew 'Black Bart' Roberts (1682–1722) pictured a pirate drinking a jug of rum with a skeleton. Although Roberts is said to have preferred to drink tea, his men were certainly fond of alcohol. This illustration shows members of Black Bart's crew partying on the coast of west Africa after a day spent making repairs to their ship.

◀ In this painting by American artist Howard Pyle (1853–1911), a gang of pirates shares out captured loot on a beach. Pirate life was surprisingly democratic. If a captain failed to carry out enough successful raids, he could be voted out of power by the crew.

Women pirates

Life for a European woman at the time of the Golden Age of piracy was generally one of obedience to men. So imagine the scandal when people read tales of female pirates, as bloodthirsty and as rule-breaking as their male counterparts! Accounts of the two most famous women pirates of the time, Mary Read and Anne Bonny, became the stuff of legend. It is likely that many other women were involved in pirate life in one way or another, although their lives were never recorded.

▲ Whatever the truth about female pirates, we know that the fate of women captured by pirates was often terrible. Movies usually tone down the historical truth about their treatment. European pirates, for example, thought nothing of torture and murder.

◄ Mary Read was portrayed as a ferocious fighter. She once fought a duel with a pirate who had insulted one of her lovers. The story goes that she ran her cutlass right through her opponent's body.

Women on board

We know that women were banned outright from some pirate ships as part of the pirate code, in case they caused fights among the crew. But having females on board ship during this era was not very unusual. Women occasionally sailed in ordinary ships as wives or mistresses of crew members, or as cooks and nurses. We know that women lived on pirate bases and it is quite possible that a number of them also went to sea in pirate ships.

Read and Bonny

Mary Read (1690–1720) and Anne Bonny (born c.1700) sailed the Caribbean alongside a pirate called 'Calico' Jack Rackham (died 1720). Disguised as a man, Mary Read had been serving as a British soldier when her ship was captured by Rackham and she joined his crew. Anne Bonny was already on board, having left her sailor husband to become Rackham's lover. Both women dressed as men and fought alongside the rest of the crew. We know about their exploits from Captain Johnson's book (see page 28) and from the records of their trial.

► While at sea, both Anne Bonny (right) and Mary Read wore men's clothing — a seaman's jacket and canvas trousers. They must have been just as strong as their male colleagues to carry the cutlass, pistols and heavy boarding axe shown in this engraving.

▲ People were fascinated by Mary Read and Anne Bonny's story. It went down in pirate history and inspired many movies that show a brave female pirate able to hold her own in a fight. This is a scene from the 1951 film *Anne of the Indies*, which was based on the exploits of Anne Bonny.

Trial and death

After taking many prizes, Rackham's ship was captured by the British navy. Only Mary and Anne put up any resistance, since the rest of the crew were drunk below deck. All those captured, including Mary and Anne, were sentenced to hang. The execution of the women was delayed, however, because they were both pregnant. Mary Read soon died of illness in a Jamaican prison, but it is said that Anne had her child, was given a pardon and left jail. What happened to her after that is a mystery.

Pirate punishments

The Golden Age of piracy began with warring European countries using pirates to harm their enemies. But when peace returned to Europe in CE1714, the seagoing nations made efforts to stamp out piracy because it was harming their growing trade with overseas colonies. Pirates became famous celebrities, who attracted large crowds to their trials and executions. By 1730, many of the most notorious pirates and their crews were dead or behind bars. The Golden Age was over.

▲ In 1718, the head of the most famous pirate of all, Blackbeard (see page 23), was cut off and hung on the front of a British navy ship to warn others not to copy him.

Hunting the criminals

British colonial governors called in the navy to help them get rid of troublesome pirates. Woodes Rogers (1679–1732) was a famous pirate hunter of the time. An ex-privateer, he became governor of the Bahamas in 1717 and set out with a Royal Navy patrol to stamp out piracy in a settlement called New Providence. He offered to pardon those pirates who gave up their life of crime, but when they broke their promise he returned and ordered a mass hanging.

The hempen jig

In England, guilty pirates were usually hanged at low tide. The body was left to be washed by the tide for a day and a half, before being cut down and buried in an unmarked grave. The most notorious criminals were covered in tar after execution and hung in chains in an iron cage to rot, as a warning to others not to take up piracy. Hanging was nicknamed the hempen jig, because victims seemed to dance on the end of the hemp rope as they jerked in their death throes.

▶ Pirate punishments were not only handed out by the authorities. A seaman who broke the pirate code could expect no mercy from his captain. For serious offences, such as running away from a fight, a pirate could be marooned on a remote desert island with little food or fresh water. The chances of rescue were slim.

▲ Pirates captured by the authorities were put in chains to stop them escaping before their trial. These leg shackles (top) and handcuffs (bottom) date from the 17th century.

Strangling and slavery

The French often sent guilty pirates to work in their colonies as slaves. The Spanish chose the garotte (strangling with a cord) as their method of pirate execution, but other grisly on-the-spot punishments were reported from time to time. In one incident, early in the 17th century, the Spanish tied captured pirates to stakes, cut off their limbs and smeared the stumps with honey. Then they left the unfortunate criminals to be eaten alive by insects.

► The famous Scottish pirate Captain William Kidd (1645–1701) was captured, tried for murder and hanged. His body was displayed in an iron cage at Tilbury Point, on the banks of the Thames estuary near London, England. The condemned man was measured for his chains before execution, so he knew what his fate would be. Kidd's rotting corpse hung there for years, as a gruesome warning to other sailors not to turn to piracy.

▲ Occasionally, pirates had to clean off barnacles and seaweed that built up on a ship's hull and slowed it down. The ship had to be pulled on to a beach for this job, called careening. It was a dangerous time for the pirate crews, so they tried to keep their careening sites a secret. There was no escape if they were caught by a navy patrol with their ship out of the water.

Chinese pirate fleets

From the 17th to the 19th centuries CE, piracy thrived in the China seas. Along China's vast coastline, countless islands and hidden estuaries made ideal pirate bases. Unlike the pirates of the Caribbean, who tended to work on their own, the Chinese worked in huge, well-organized fleets. They used violent threats to blackmail money from coastal settlements and merchant ships. The piracy business became so important that its leaders ruled over large areas, like mini-emperors.

▼ The junk was the all-purpose ship of both merchant and pirate fleets in the China seas. The basic design was simple, with three masts carrying sails made of bamboo matting. Many pirate junks were trading ships that had been captured and converted. They were armed with cannon and swivel-guns called lantaka. The larger junks could carry up to 200 crew, and were more than a match for the ships of the Chinese navy.

▲ In 1849, a large pirate fleet led by Chui Apoo (died 1851) was hunted down and destroyed off the coast of China by British naval gunboats. A navy ship can be seen in the centre of this painting, with its distinctive, European-style square sails.

Criminal fleets

In the mid-17th century, a pirate leader called Cheng Chih Lung (dates unknown) built up a fleet of several hundred ships that controlled much of the Chinese coast. The Chinese emperor, recognizing his power, made him an admiral in the navy – with responsibility for hunting pirates! More than a century later, the pirate chief Ching-I (1784–1844) commanded about 30,000 crew in the biggest pirate fleet that ever sailed. His fleet was organized into six squadrons, each with its own area of operation. It was, in effect, a floating criminal army.

A family business

Piracy in the China seas was a family affair. Most pirate captains sailed with their wives and family on board. Pirate leaders employed family members in their businesses, and it was common for relatives to inherit a fleet when a captain died. When Cheng Chih Lung was betrayed and killed by the emperor, his son, Kuo Hsing Yeh (1624–1662), took over his father's fleet. He drove the official naval forces out of his territory and built up a vast trading empire.

Steam-powered pirate hunting

The opium drug trade between China and Europe was very profitable, and the British sent their navy to protect it from piracy. The final showdown came in 1849, when a joint Royal Navy and Chinese force fought the notorious Shap'ng-Tsai (dates unknown) off the coast of Vietnam. The steam-powered British warships were the most formidable in the world. They trapped the pirate fleet, bombarded and destroyed it. Shap'ng-Tsai escaped, but it was the end of the pirate fleets.

▲ Chinese pirates traditionally fought with a large two-handed sword, while Japanese pirates fought with a smaller sword in each hand. But western weapons also came into use, as shown in this picture of a Japanese pirate chief holding a revolver.

▶ The islands of Indonesia and the Philippines provided safe refuge for pirates, as they still do today (see pages 52–53). The inlets and islands of Borneo and Sumatra (shown here) sheltered fierce, head-hunting pirate tribes.

Political pirates

Although the Golden Age of piracy had ended, the upheavals of the Revolutionary War (1775–83) and the Napoleonic Wars (1799–1815) saw another surge in piracy, this time driven by politics. The American and French navies were not strong enough to take on the British Royal Navy alone, so they hired privateers to harass the British merchant fleet and disrupt trade.

▲ This photograph shows Haiti-born pirate Jean Lafitte as a romantic hero in a 1938 film, *The Buccaneer*.

Privateers for independence

In CE1775, at the outset of the Revolutionary War between Britain and its American colonies, the American navy had barely 30 ships. So the Americans licensed privateers to attack British merchant vessels. Operating from Atlantic ports such as Boston and Baltimore, they devastated British trade to the Americas, seizing almost 3,000 ships. At one time, up to 500 privateers were regularly attacking the British merchant fleet.

▼ John Paul Jones' greatest feat was the capture in 1779 of the British 50-gun warship *Serapis* in the North Sea. Jones' ship, the *Bonhomme Richard*, was a converted merchant vessel. Uncertain of the state of his cannon, he decided to fight the *Serapis* at close quarters. The battle was so vicious that Jones' own vessel eventually sank, but not before the captain of the severely damaged *Serapis* had surrendered.

Scourge of the British

The Scotsman John Paul Jones (1747–92) was viewed as a pirate by the British, but he was a hero to the Americans. Working as an officer in the American navy, he sailed to Europe in 1778 to attack British ships. France supported the Americans in the Revolutionary War, so Jones was allowed to operate from French Channel ports. He captured merchant vessels and even landed on the coast of northwestern England, destroying shipping in the port of Whitehaven.

Pirate or hero?

Jean Lafitte (c.1780–c.1825) was a pirate who operated on both sides of the law. In the early 1800s, he was based in Barataria Bay, south of New Orleans, USA, illegally smuggling and slave-trading. His pirate fleet was raided by a US naval force in 1814, but a year later he won a pardon for helping the city of New Orleans to defeat a British attempt to capture it. Lafitte was a national hero for a while, until he stole a ship and sailed to Texas to carry on his life of piracy.

French corsairs

During the Napoleonic Wars, Britain fought France and blockaded the French navy in its home ports. France hit back at the British using privateers called corsairs. They operated from French Channel ports such as St Malo and Dunkerque, which had been pirate haunts for centuries. They captured up to 2,000 British merchant ships during the early years of the wars. Thanks to their raids, the French corsairs became national heroes and very rich men.

◄ Robert Surcouf (1773–1827), portrayed here in the film *The Sea Pirate*, was one of the most famous French corsairs of Napoleonic times. He attacked British shipping in the Indian Ocean.

Secretive smugglers

Smuggling across the English Channel was common during the 18th and 19th centuries CE. To finance its many wars of the time, the British government demanded the payment of high taxes, called duty, on luxury goods that were imported from abroad, such as brandy and tea. The tax demands were so heavy that smuggling grew into a large industry. The smuggled goods – known as contraband – were secretly shipped to remote parts of the British coast to avoid paying money to government tax agents, or revenue men.

Night-time deliveries

Smuggling boats arrived on the English coast under cover of night. Gang members on land would signal to the ships when the coast was clear of revenue men. The smugglers would then bring the cargo to shore, and the gang would carry the goods off the beach to be hidden. Smuggling ships were light and fast, and they had sails that allowed them to move with or against the wind. This was vital if they had to come in close to shore and get away quickly to avoid capture. The boats were usually painted black, with dark sails as night-time camouflage.

Secret cargoes

The smugglers' most popular cargoes were brandy, gin, tobacco, tea, and silk and lace for fine clothes. Wealthy British people would buy these luxuries without asking where they came from, and the smugglers' profits were high. Brandy and gin were smuggled in small barrels that could be hidden easily on a ship. Tobacco was packed into small, waterproof bundles. In an emergency, the tobacco would be thrown overboard into the sea. Because they floated, the bundles could be picked up later by gang members in rowing boats.

◀ In this dramatic illustration, smugglers are attacked by revenue men (in blue jackets). Many violent battles were fought between the two groups. Smugglers fought hard to escape capture and punishment.

COWAN'S

Nº 4 fine old

BELFAST

IRISH WHISKY

No 4

Smuggling killers

Whole communities were involved in smuggling, as it took lots of people to land and hide a cargo. It was also safer that way. If all the locals profited from the trade, they were more likely to stay quiet about it. Some smuggling gangs used violent threats to ensure silence. The most notorious was the Hawkhurst Gang, which operated on the Romney marshes of southeastern England. Seven of its leaders were hanged in 1749 after the torture and murder of a custom's official and a shoemaker. The official was buried alive, and the shoemaker was thrown into a well.

▲ In this advertisement from 1891, smugglers are landing a barrel of smuggled whisky on a deserted beach. They are shown as cheerful, harmless rogues, but in reality smugglers were often violent and dangerous criminals.

▼ After the mid-1700s, captured British smugglers were usually hanged only if they had murdered someone. Instead, many were transported. This meant they were sent to British colonies overseas, such as Australia, to work as slaves. While they waited to sail, prisoners were sometimes kept in prison hulks – rotting, stinking old ships that were anchored close to shore. This painting from 1828 shows a prison hulk in Portsmouth harbour, on the south coast of England.

Smuggling tales and truth

The English Channel is the setting for smuggling legends that date back to the 18th century CE. Many of them tell how the smugglers tried to trick the authorities to avoid capture. As with piracy, these smuggling stories have fuelled the imaginations of writers and movie makers. Romantic myths have built up around secret tunnels, murderous wreckers and aristocratic criminal masterminds.

▲ Smugglers regularly criss-crossed the English Channel, carrying a wide variety of cargoes. The French emperor Napoleon I (1769–1821) had supplies of gold smuggled from England to finance his wars.

Hiding the stash

Smugglers used many clever tricks to hide contraband. Tobacco was woven into rope and piled innocently on deck. Brandy and gin were smuggled in secret compartments built into the bottom of ordinary water barrels. When revenue men began to measure the depth of the barrels, the smugglers built tapering compartments so that the sides of the barrel held the spirits while the barrel depth seemed normal.

Pits were sometimes dug at the top of a beach to hide a smuggled cargo until it could be moved out. These had to be very deep, because revenue men poked long probes into the sand to look for them. Specially built smuggling tunnels were much more rare, but there is an example at Hayle, in Cornwall, southwestern England. It runs for several hundred metres from the coast to the town.

▼ According to legend, villagers living on the coast of Cornwall would steal the washed-up cargoes of ships that had been wrecked in storms. It was even rumoured that surviving crew members would be murdered, and their valuables stolen.

Cunning criminals

Smugglers laid careful plans for landing a cargo. Often, if the coast was not clear, the smuggling ship would sail to one of several alternative landing points. Smugglers built coastal houses with special towers or high windows from which a pre-arranged light signal could be made. They also made lanterns which concentrated the light in a beam out to sea, but not to the countryside around.

Master smugglers

Smugglers needed financial backers because it was expensive to buy the cargo abroad. Shadowy figures financed the illegal trade and made fortunes, particularly in the southeast of England, close to the London markets. As with the drug trade today, they were rarely identified or brought to justice. It was the people who actually carried out the smuggling who were caught and punished.

▶ Many of Cornwall's smuggling tales feature wreckers — villagers who deliberately wrecked ships near the shore. They lit beacons to fool a vessel's crew into thinking they were close to port when, in fact, they were being guided on to rocks.

SUMMARY OF CHAPTER 2: THE GOLDEN AGE

A ship's cannon dating
from the Golden Age

The legend of the Golden Age pirate

Writers turned the pirates of the Golden Age into anti-heroes – bad but fascinating characters. They based their stories on the reports of eyewitnesses who told of the extraordinary adventures and wicked cruelties of men such as Blackbeard, Henry Morgan and William Kidd. We cannot tell how true some of the writings were, but we do know that colourful reports of pirate lives and deaths sold well, and were the inspiration for many vivid pirate legends.

Pirates, smugglers and politics

The Golden Age of piracy lasted for just 40 years, roughly from CE1690 to 1730. As Europe became more peaceful at the end of the 17th century, rulers no longer needed their privateer forces – but the pirates continued to attack cargo ships because the profits were so high. But now the pirates were harming the trade of the governments they once aided, so they were hunted down and punished.

Smuggling in the Golden Age grew out of politics too. It was a way of avoiding the heavy tax that governments placed on imported goods to help pay for their wars.

The truth

In reality, pirates of the 17th and 18th centuries were criminals who murdered innocent people at sea and terrorized communities on land. Smugglers of the time could also be very violent, using threats and even torture to silence people who witnessed their crimes.

In addition, the Golden Age buccaneers and pirates helped to start the slave trade that forced millions of Africans to work against their will in the Americas. But there is no doubt that they also led extraordinary lives that will continue to fascinate us for centuries to come.

Go further...

The Pirate's Realm is packed with fascinating information, games and a list of all the pirate museums around the world, with links:
www.thepiratesrealm.com

Read *Treasure Island*, the classic pirate adventure, written by Robert Louis Stevenson (Penguin). *Moonfleet* is an action-packed smuggling tale by John Meade Falkner (Penguin).

Pirates! by Celia Rees (Bloomsbury, 2004)

The World of Ships by Philip Wilkinson (Kingfisher, 2005)

Eyewitness Guides: Pirate by Richard Platt (Dorling Kindersley, 2002)

Film scriptwriter
Writes the script for a movie, including all the actors' lines and action scenes.

Historian
Reads and writes about people, places and events from the past.

Prop and costume maker
Creates historical costumes and artefacts, often for use in films and television programmes.

Researcher
Studies a particular area of history, looking through old documents and accounts for historical clues. May also advise film and television programme makers.

Cornwall, in the far southwest of the UK, has many smuggling coves and inns. You can also visit the National Maritime Museum Cornwall: Discovery Quay, Falmouth TR11 3QY, UK Telephone: +44 (0) 1326 313388
www.nmmc.co.uk

The eastern coast of the USA is dotted with maritime museums. These include:

The New England Pirate Museum, 274 Derby Street, Salem, USA
www.piratemuseum.com

The Mel Fisher Museum, 200 Greene Street, Key West, USA
www.melfisher.org

Refugees, such as these Vietnamese people, often fall victim to modern-day pirates and smugglers (see pages 50–51)

CHAPTER 3

Modern piracy and smuggling

Piracy and smuggling are not simply crimes from past centuries. They are flourishing today, and are often organized by vicious international crime gangs, such as the Mafia and the Chinese Triads.

Piracy grows year-by-year, particularly around Nigeria and parts of southeast Asia. Today's pirates have fast boats, high-tech equipment and machine guns. They prey on merchant shipping and yachts, stealing from the crew and sometimes even capturing a whole ship and its cargo.

Smuggling is a major modern crime too. Drugs, people and wildlife have replaced alcohol and tobacco as the main cargoes in this illegal activity.

Rum runners

In the 1920s, alcohol was made illegal in the USA. This era was known as Prohibition, and it caused a steep rise in alcohol smuggling by sea. Illegal cargoes of rum and whisky were landed along the Atlantic and Pacific coasts of the USA and then transported to big cities for secret sale. The smugglers were nicknamed rum runners. It was a very lucrative trade that attracted violent gangsters, such as Al Capone.

▲ This 1921 magazine illustration shows US authorities destroying smuggled alcohol by pouring it down a drain. The police might have captured some of it by raiding illegal bars called speakeasies.

Rum row

Fleets of large vessels heavily laden with alcohol would sail towards the USA but anchor perfectly legally outside the 5km territorial limit around the coast. Smaller boats would sail out to them, load up with cargo and smuggle it back to the coast. A line of big ships anchored at sea was called a rum row, and this could mean up to 14 vessels. At first, riotous parties were held on the rum row ships. People sailed or even rowed out to them from the shore for a drunken night out, as well as a spot of smuggling. Later, the territorial limit was changed to 19km out from the shore, and rum running became much harder.

Gangsters get involved

Prohibition was unpopular, and many Americans were prepared to buy alcohol secretly – so the smugglers made a lot of money. At first the rum runners were a mixed bunch of sailors and fishermen, but then gangster mobs took over. They drove ordinary boatmen from the trade with threats, violence, and even murder. Rum running became a deadly chase between coastguard boats and gangster vessels, both armed with deck-mounted machine guns.

◀ These torpedoes, which are full of alcohol, were confiscated from a rum row schooner (a small, fast sailing ship). They were designed to be shot from the schooner, collected, and then dragged to shore by smaller boats. Smuggling alcohol during Prohibition was known as bootlegging.

Tricks of the trade

Rum-running boats often had false bottoms for hiding alcohol. On fishing boats, a layer of fish might cover up the real cargo, and one rum runner even designed a vehicle that he could load up with alcohol and tow behind his boat to look like fishing equipment. The gangsters built fast, armour-plated boats to outrun the coastguard, with the powerful engines muffled to be as quiet as possible. Sometimes they fitted devices that poured oily smoke into the path of a chasing coastguard boat.

▶ The notorious US gangster Al Capone (1899–1947) was involved in rum running. He was a 'mobster' – the leader of a violent organized crime gang that ran many illegal businesses. The mobsters made big profits from alcohol smuggling. The law-breaking became so bad that Prohibition was ended in 1933.

▼ Prohibition law-enforcement agents examine confiscated cases of whisky on board a coastguard ship. Boat chases often took place on foggy nights, when the smugglers tried to land their goods unseen.

Modern-day smuggling

Ocean-going smuggling still takes place around the world. Smugglers make big profits by avoiding government taxes on imported goods, by bringing in illegal cargo, such as drugs, and by smuggling people between countries. Heavily armed and violent gangs are often involved, as they have been for centuries.

▲ In 2001, British port police found the drug heroin hidden inside thousands of individual almond nuts. The drugs, worth four million UK pounds, had been shipped from Sri Lanka.

Deadly cargoes

Tobacco and alcohol are still smuggled by sea to avoid paying duty, or import tax, to governments – just as they were in centuries gone by. Today, however, larger profits are made from smuggling drugs and arms (weapons). Innocent-looking sailing yachts may conceal cargoes of cocaine or heroin to be sold for high prices on city streets. Arms are illegally smuggled to war zones, or for use by criminals.

Speedy smugglers

Nowadays, smugglers use lightweight 'go-fast' boats to get their cargo to shore. These are usually fitted with several engines so that they can reach top speeds in a chase. Because the boats are built with no metallic fittings, they cannot be detected by radar except at close range or in a calm sea. The best way for coastguards to catch go-fast boats is to spot them from above, by helicopter.

Smuggling hotspots

The world's biggest drug producers are found in South America and Asia, but the major drug markets are in North America and Europe (see map below). To move the drugs from one country to another involves smuggling them undetected across borders, often through ports or boat marinas. The Gulf of Mexico is a smuggling hotspot, just as it was in the days of Jean Lafitte (see page 37). Drugs and arms are brought by sea from Central America, through the Gulf to isolated spots on the southern US coast.

A violent crime

Modern smuggling often involves violence. Criminals double-cross each other, use threats to scare people into keeping quiet, and are heavily armed to resist arrest. The penalties for drug smuggling are high. In some countries, the automatic punishment is death.

THE WORLD'S MAJOR SMUGGLING ROUTES

KEY
→ People
→ Wildlife
→ Drugs

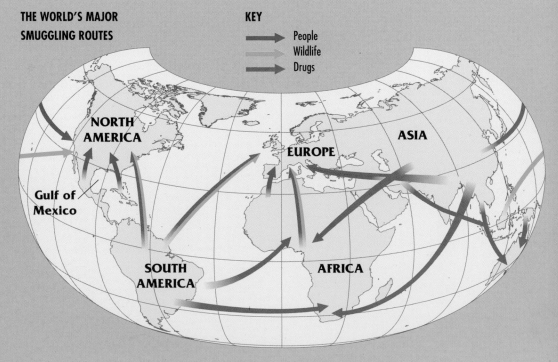

NORTH AMERICA

Gulf of Mexico

SOUTH AMERICA

EUROPE

ASIA

AFRICA

► Customs officers use fast, inflatable boats, called RHIs (rigid-hulled inflatables), to chase down drug-smuggling vessels. The lightweight RHIs can reach a top speed of up to 90km/h. They are equipped with radar and, in some countries, several types of weapons.

Wildlife smugglers

Wildlife is now the third most profitable smuggling cargo after drugs and arms. The Worldwide Fund for Nature estimates that criminal gangs could be making profits of up to a staggering 20 billion US dollars each year from smuggling live animals and rare plants to unscrupulous collectors. The criminals do not care about bringing rare creatures close to extinction or causing them terrible suffering on their illegal journeys.

Smuggling from South America

Up to 11 million animals a year are smuggled from South America, mostly to the USA, where they are sold illegally to collectors over the internet or through corrupt dealers. Many highly endangered animals are under threat from smugglers, including rare parrots, monkeys and snakes. But, out of every ten animals captured for smuggling, it is estimated that only one survives the journey to become an exotic pet.

▶ The rare and beautiful red-tailed black cockatoo is a type of parrot. It is protected by law in Australia, but some collectors pay up to US$25,000 for a smuggled specimen.

◀ These macaque monkeys are chained up for sale in an Asian market. Some kidnapped animals are lucky enough to be rescued from markets and returned to the wild, but most die in captivity.

Big profits from cruelty

Rare animals that survive smuggling make bigger profits for criminals than smuggled drugs. An Amazonian blue macaw might sell for US$25,000, for instance, and an endangered tamarin monkey can fetch US$20,000. Gangs have been known to combine both trades by hiding drugs inside rare animals. In one example, smuggled snakes from Colombia were forced to swallow cocaine-filled bags. Customs officers discovered the snakes and noticed the unusual bulges inside them. Sadly, many of the snakes died from swallowing the drugs.

The fight against smugglers

Rare animals are often transported by boat through busy ports, where it is difficult for the authorities to check every cargo. The police try to track the movements of smuggling gangs by talking to local contacts and combing street markets where illegally captured animals are sold. They also investigate pet dealers and websites to find out who is buying the animals.

From orchids to ivory

Modern smugglers make money from all sorts of goods. Rare orchids are illegally dug up and smuggled from countries such as New Zealand and Peru. Caviar, one of the world's most expensive foods, is smuggled from Russia. Rare tigers are illegally killed and their body parts sold in Asia as an ingredient in traditional medicines. Elephants and rhinos are killed for their ivory tusks, which are used in medicines and carvings.

▶ Rare orchids have been prized by collectors for their exotic beauty since the 19th century. There are more than 25,000 different kinds of orchid. This is a lady's slipper, one of the most commonly smuggled types.

◀ Reptiles and insects make big profits for smugglers. Chameleons, such as this panther chameleon from the African island of Madagascar, are illegally caught and sold to collectors as pets.

Smuggling people

People smuggling is growing rapidly across the world. Organized criminal gangs smuggle large numbers of people illegally across country borders by boat, truck or plane. They make big profits by charging for the dangerous trip, and also by threatening or blackmailing their clients.

Why people pay

In some countries, many poor people are willing to pay all the money they have to criminal gangs that will smuggle them across the border. Their destinations are wealthier nations, such as Britain, Australia and the USA, where they can start a new life. They may want to work in a country where wages are higher, or to escape violence, war or political oppression in their own lands.

Threats and blackmail

Once people have been transported illegally into a country, they are often threatened by the smugglers and forced to work for criminals, passing on their earnings and taking part in crime themselves. If they refuse they may be killed, or their relatives back home may be threatened with violence. The smuggled people find themselves in a trap, unable to tell the police what is happening to them.

Dangerous journey

People who move from one country to another are known as migrants. Smuggled migrants face a hazardous journey. The smugglers cram hundreds of people on to dirty, unsafe boats, often without proper food. The crews may be violent and sometimes throw sick people into the sea. In some areas of southeast Asia, the smugglers' boats even run the risk of being attacked by murderous pirates.

▲ In the late 1990s, a war in the Balkan region of Europe led to thousands of refugees flooding into other European countries. These people are fleeing from Kosovo to Albania. Wars often lead to a rise in people smuggling, as refugees try to find a better life elsewhere.

▼ A US coastguard vessel intercepts a boat crammed with illegal migrants from the Caribbean country of Haiti. Most of them will have paid criminals to get them on to the boat, in the hope of making a new life in the USA.

Risking everything

One of the world's people-smuggling hotspots is the Strait of Gibraltar. This narrow strip of sea, between Morocco and Spain, separates Africa and Europe by only 13km. Migrants squeeze on to small, overcrowded boats to make the crossing. People who fall overboard often drown in the dangerous, fast-flowing currents. Another busy smuggling route runs from China to Europe. Migrants pay Chinese gangs to cram them into trucks or even ship containers for long and often fatal journeys.

▶ An illegal migrant held by police at Tarifa, a town facing Morocco on the coast of southern Spain. Migrants regularly land here by boat, often brought across the Strait of Gibraltar by criminal gangs.

Pirates today

Piracy did not die out with the likes of Blackbeard. Today, it is a growing crime that is increasingly well organized and violent. Heavily armed pirates attack merchant ships and yachts in fast boats, terrorizing the crew or murdering them, then stealing what they can. Piracy is a particular problem in Indonesia, Bangladesh, Vietnam, India, Nigeria, and the ports and rivers of Brazil.

▼ These Filipino pirates are using a flat-bottomed canoe that can move fast and is also useful in shallow waters. They are armed with powerful rifles. In 2003, 20 sailors were reported to have been killed by pirates worldwide. Many more deaths may go unreported.

◄ Isolated coastal villages, in places such as the Philippines, sometimes shelter pirate gangs that threaten passing vessels.

Dangerous waters

The Malacca Strait – a narrow strip of water between Indonesia, Singapore and Malaysia – is said to be the world's most dangerous shipping route. Here, there are rich pickings for pirate gangs that hide among the many islands. More than a quarter of the world's cargo ships pass through the Strait every year, including many oil tankers. These and other large merchant ships have small crews that are easily overpowered by swarms of armed gunmen.

Speedy attack

Modern pirates tend to hide in inlets and on islands. They speed out to surprise their prey, disguised in masks and armed with automatic rifles. They may steal from local fishermen or yachts, or attack larger merchant ships to steal the cargo and valuables on board. Occasionally, they take over a ship and demand a ransom for the safe return of the crew.

▲ Major ports are hotbeds of smuggling and piracy. The ports of Brazil, such as Santos (above), are amongst the most dangerous in the world, along with the ports of Indonesia and Bangladesh. Every month, millions of dollars-worth of illegal goods and stolen cargo are smuggled through these ports, with the help of corrupt officials.

Piracy and corruption

Sophisticated gangs use high-tech methods to steal from merchant ships in the Malacca Strait. They plan raids on specific cargoes, using inside information from unscrupulous office workers in shipping companies. They intercept e-mails and telephone calls to find out what the cargoes are, how many crew members a ship is carrying, and what the route will be. Corrupt government officials help the gangs to hide their crime and sell the stolen cargo.

Amazon attack

In 2001, river piracy hit the headlines when the famous yachtsman Sir Peter Blake (1948–2001) was killed by bandits who raided his boat on the Amazon river in Brazil.

Catching the criminals

Coastguard crews and port police are at the front line of law enforcement, trying to catch smugglers both in ports and out at sea. They use well-equipped boats and surveillance planes for this dangerous job. On an average day, US coastguards search up to 140 vessels and seize narcotics (drugs) worth around US$10.8 million.

▲ Narcotics worth billions of dollars are smuggled into the USA every year. Many of these illegal drugs are hidden in ships and brought into the country through ports. This means that the port police have to be on the lookout for suspect cargo at all times. In this drugs bust in Miami, in 2003, police found a huge haul.

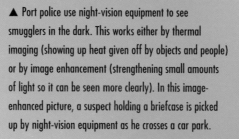

▲ Port police use night-vision equipment to see smugglers in the dark. This works either by thermal imaging (showing up heat given off by objects and people) or by image enhancement (strengthening small amounts of light so it can be seen more clearly). In this image-enhanced picture, a suspect holding a briefcase is picked up by night-vision equipment as he crosses a car park.

Dangerous work

Coastguard policing can be a very risky business. In the past, smugglers often fought government officials, sometimes even murdering them. Today, the danger is still great, and so coastguard police are highly trained to cope with armed criminals who resist arrest. Good police work relies on information. This may come from law-enforcement officers who work undercover to find out about criminal gangs and illegal shipments.

Port searches

If customs officers suspect that a ship docked in port is carrying illegally smuggled cargo, they will search it using a range of equipment. They might use sniffer dogs trained to find drugs, or screen the boat with radiation and explosive detectors. To find stowaway migrants, they use devices that measure the level of carbon dioxide gas in cargo containers. If the level is high, it could be a sign that people are inside, as humans breathe out carbon dioxide.

Customs cutters

Coastguards use cutters (a boat over 20 metres long) for coastal patrols. On board, there is often a smaller boat such as an RHI (see page 47), which the customs officers use to approach and board any vessel they want to search. The cutters are often equipped with powerful computers for tracking and navigation, as well as surface radar and other high-tech apparatus, to pinpoint vessels at sea.

Police to the rescue

As well as fast boats, coastguard police use surveillance planes and helicopters to help them find boats at sea. Small vessels full of illegal migrants can most easily be seen from above. They are usually unsafe and dangerously overcrowded, and may get into difficulties. The migrants' only chance of survival might be for a coastguard plane to spot their boat and launch a rescue.

▲ Rescue helicopters are called out by the coastguard if a boat carrying illegal migrants gets into trouble. Coastguards also have their own spotter helicopters. In some countries these have armed officers on board, ready to shoot at the engines of suspicious-looking boats, putting them out of action.

▼ Sniffer dogs can detect drugs ten times faster than humans are able to. Some dogs are cross-trained – this means they can detect hidden people as well as drugs. In this picture, the face of the dog handler has been blurred to protect her identity from smugglers.

Wreck hunters

Underwater archaeologists study shipwrecks to find clues about the people who once lived on board. Some wrecks also contain valuable treasure that can be sold at auction, and that is why many underwater treasure hunters get involved in wreck hunting. In recent years, as underwater technology has become more sophisticated, some exciting finds have been made on sunken pirate ships.

Locating a shipwreck

It is not easy to find a wrecked ship. Researchers spend many hours in libraries and archives, where old documents and records are kept. They read historical letters, journals and maps to spot clues that point to the area where a ship sank. However, a wreck might be buried, or broken up and spread over a wide area. To track down the exact location, wreck hunters use special equipment to carry out a survey. For example, the sea floor can be mapped using magnetometers, which detect metal objects, and sonar equipment, which picks out shapes on the sea bed.

▲ A ship's logbook (background image) can be a valuable tool to wreck hunters. This example dates from ce1790.

▼ These divers are at work in waters off the Bahamas, in the Caribbean. They are using an air-filled balloon to raise to the surface a heavy iron cannon from the 17th-century Spanish ship *Nuestra Señora de las Maravillas*.

► Once the remains of a ship have been pinpointed, divers begin the painstaking job of measuring, mapping, sketching and taking photographs of the wreck.

Protecting the wreck

The people who discover a wreck usually have salvage rights over it, which means they can claim what they find. But illegal wreck hunters often arrive to raid a site of its treasures, and in doing so they may damage valuable historical evidence. That is why wreck hunters try to keep a site secret for as long as possible.

Finding objects

First, a survey is made of the wreck site. It is important to record exactly where objects are found, because that might help archaeologists decide how items were used and who owned them. Divers then use metal detectors, probes and their hands to make finds. Often, they clear away mud and sand using pipes that suck up the dirt like a vacuum cleaner.

Finds are lifted very carefully to the surface. Objects brought up from the sea bed rot rapidly in fresh air. They must be kept wet, or they crumble before they can be preserved.

◄ These underwater archaeologists are examining a hoard of Spanish coins they have just recovered from the wreck of the pirate ship *Whydah*, off the coast of Cape Cod, USA.

▲ This shoe was recovered from the pirate ship *Whydah*, which was captained by Samuel 'Black Sam' Bellamy (died 1717). Divers also found a human leg bone that was still clothed in a silk stocking.

▶ If a wreck lies in very deep water, scuba divers are unable to swim down to it. Instead, submersibles are sent to explore the remains. A famous example of this is the *Titanic*, which sank in the Atlantic Ocean in 1912. It lies at a depth of around 4km, and only a few manned submersibles can reach it. This is the Russian submersible *Mir I*, just after a trip down to the *Titanic*.

Patient preservation

Preservation and restoration work on the finds from a wreck can take many years and a lot of patience. Wood has to be washed over and over again to get rid of the sea salt. Then it is soaked in chemicals to stop it rotting, and barnacles are gently removed. Metal objects corrode (rot away) underwater, but on land this crumbling can be stopped by putting the find in a tank of water and passing an electrical current through it.

Fine dressers

The first ever pirate shipwreck to be found and explored was the *Whydah*, which sank off the coast of the USA during a howling storm in 1717. The finds included thousands of coins, as well as personal items that tell us much about the pirates who lived on board. For instance, belt buckles, buttons and jewellery suggest that the crew liked to dress finely.

All washed up

Since the wreck of the *Whydah* was discovered in 1984, more exciting pirate ship finds have been made. Wreck hunters have located vessels off the US coast that belonged to Captain Morgan and Blackbeard. In 1996, a wreck thought to be a Barbary pirate ship was discovered after some Arab coins were washed up on a beach in Salcombe Bay, southern England. Perhaps the pirates were on their way to raid the coast for slaves.

◀ This hoard of treasure, now kept in the British Museum, London, was recovered by divers from the sea bed in Salcombe Bay. In total, the collection includes over 400 gold coins, broken pieces of gold jewellery, pottery shards and a merchant's seal. No one knows the identity of the ship that carried the treasure, but it may have been a Barbary pirate vessel.

SUMMARY OF CHAPTER 3: MODERN PIRACY AND SMUGGLING

From local to international

In the past, smuggling was carried out by local gangs as a way of cheating the government of import tax. In contrast, modern smugglers are highly organized criminals who have contacts around the world. Law-enforcement agencies work internationally too, co-operating to try to stop the harm that these crimes cause. The smuggling of people, drugs and wildlife involves cruelty and misery on a much greater scale than ever before.

Today's pirates may be local fishermen who boost their income by stealing valuable goods, or they may be criminal gangs trying to make a big profit quickly.

High-tech crime

Modern pirates and smugglers have high-tech equipment, such as night-vision goggles and satellite navigation systems. They use the latest weapons and high-speed boats. The crime-busting authorities have to be just as well equipped to have any chance of catching the criminals. Governments spend large sums of money on coastguard patrols and vessel searches.

High-tech discoveries

Underwater archaeologists are using newly developed high-tech equipment to make exciting discoveries. They are bringing shipwreck stories to life, by raising to the surface objects that have been lost for centuries on the sea bed. Their fascinating finds tell us a great deal about the hazardous and often brutal lives of the pirates and smugglers of the past.

A small submarine used by Colombian drug smugglers in the 1990s

Go further...

For a list of all the reconstructed or restored ships that you can visit around the world, go to:
www.ils.unc.edu/maritime/ships.shtml

To go piracy and shipwreck websurfing, visit:
http://yahooligans.yahoo.com
Then type in 'shipwrecks' or 'pirates' to get a long list of fun, kid-friendly sites to check out.

Discover more about endangered species of animals and plants on the Red List database:
www.redlist.org

Coastguard watch officer
Monitors the movements of ships, and may be involved in sea rescues.

Customs officer
Fights illegal smuggling by searching people, vehicles and cargoes at ports and airports.

Diver
Trains to dive safely in the ocean, perhaps to work on historical wrecks.

Lifeboat crew member
Volunteer who comes to the aid of ships that are in difficulty at sea.

Oceanographer
Studies the oceans of the world, including wildlife and the sea bed.

Objects from the wreck of the *Whydah* are on display at the Expedition *Whydah* Sea Lab and Learning Centre: Macmillan Wharf, Provincetown, USA
www.whydah.com

To find out the location and website address of your nearest maritime museum, go to:
www.maritimemuseums.net

Visit the British Museum to see coins, jewellery and pottery recovered from the Salcombe Bay wreck site:
Great Russell Street, London WC1B 3DG, UK
Telephone: +44 (0) 20 7323 8000
www.thebritishmuseum.ac.uk

Glossary

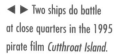

◄ ► Two ships do battle at close quarters in the 1995 pirate film *Cutthroat Island*.

aft Towards the back (stern) of a ship.

antiseptic A substance that kills germs and prevents infections.

arms Weapons.

barbarian An uncivilized and violent person.

Barbary pirate A Muslim pirate from the coast of north Africa.

bowsprit A long mast sticking out from the front of a sailing ship.

buccaneer A pirate who attacked Spanish ships in the Americas during the 17th century CE.

careening Cleaning the barnacles off a ship's hull.

cargo The goods being carried by a ship.

city-state A political system in which an independent city rules over the surrounding countryside. Ancient Greece was made up of many city-states.

coastguard Coastline police and rescue services.

colony Land claimed and settled by another country.

contraband Smuggled goods.

corsair A French word for a privateer or pirate. Also the name given to a Barbary pirate.

cutlass A short sword with a wide blade.

doubloon A Spanish gold coin.

duty A government tax on luxury goods, such as tobacco, brought into a country from abroad.

fore Towards the front of a ship.

forecastle A raised deck at the front of a ship.

galleon A large, slow and sturdy treasure ship, used by the Spanish from the 1500s to the 1700s.

galley A boat powered by both sails and rows of oarsmen.

go-fast boat A small, fast, modern boat. It has a lightweight, V-shaped hull made from fibreglass.

Golden Age The period roughly between CE1690 and 1730, when piracy was common off the coast of America and in the Indian Ocean.

harem A group of wives kept by a Muslim ruler.

hempen jig The nickname pirates gave to hanging.

hulk An old ship used as a prison.

hull The outer shell of a ship.

import To buy or bring in goods from another country.

Jolly Roger A flag used by pirates to signal an attack.

junk An Asian ship with sails made of bamboo matting.

keel A ship's lowest timber, running the full length of the vessel and supporting the entire frame of the hull.

Knights of St John A band of Christian knights, formed in the early 12th century CE.

lateen sail A triangular sail, used on Arab boats.

letter of marque A licence given to a sailor, granting him or her permission to attack enemy ships. *See also* privateer.

magnetometer An instrument that measures the magnetic field of an object. It can be used underwater to detect metal objects buried below the sea bed.

merchant ship A ship carrying cargo to sell.

migrant A person who moves from one country to another.

musket An early type of gun, with a long barrel.

Muslim A person who follows the religion of Islam.

mutiny A rebellion against authority. In a mutiny at sea, ordinary sailors would take over the ship from their captain.

narcotics Drugs.

opium A drug made from the seeds of the poppy flower.

Ottoman Empire The Turkish empire in Europe, Africa and Asia that lasted from the 13th century CE to 1923.

piece of eight A Spanish silver coin.

piracy Robbery at sea, stealing or destroying ships, and raiding settlements along a coast.

pirate code A list of rules that pirate crews agreed to obey.

pirate round A voyage from the Americas to west Africa and the Indian Ocean, and back again.

political oppression The bad treatment of someone because of their political beliefs.

poop deck A raised deck at the back of a ship.

privateer A sailor given a licence by a country's government to attack the ships of an enemy.

prize A ship stolen by a pirate.

Prohibition A law banning the sale of alcohol in the USA during the 1920s. It led to smuggling.

radar A system for tracking objects using radio signals.

ransom A fee demanded for the release of a captured person.

rapier A long, narrow, two-edged sword, popular in the 16th and 17th centuries CE.

refugee A person who has escaped from danger or a problem, often by moving from one country to another.

revenue men British tax officials.

rigging The network of ropes that help to hold up a ship's masts and that allow the sails to be controlled.

rudder A large, flat structure fixed by hinges to the rear of a ship, and turned to steer the vessel.

rum runner Someone who smuggled alcohol into the USA during the years of Prohibition.

scurvy A disease of the skin and gums caused by a lack of vitamin C in a person's diet. It can be prevented by eating citrus fruit.

sloop A small, fast ship with one mast and a triangular sail.

smuggler A person who breaks the law by transporting goods or people secretly from one country to another.

sonar A system that uses sound signals to measure the depth of an object in water.

Spanish Main The Spanish colonies of the Caribbean, Central America and the shores of South America.

stern The rear of a ship.

transportation A punishment in which criminals were sent to a faraway colony as slaves.

Viking One of the Scandinavian warriors who invaded Europe between the 8th and 11th centuries CE.

weevil A type of beetle.

Index

Acknowledgements

The publisher would like to thank the following for permission to reproduce their material. Every care has been taken to trace copyright holders. However, if there have been unintentional omissions or failure to trace copyright holders, we apologize and will, if informed, endeavour to make corrections in any future edition.

Key: *b* = bottom, *c* = centre, *l* = left, *r* = right, *t* = top

Cover *l* Corbis/Joel W. Rogers; cover *c* Corbis/Archivo Iconografico, S.A.; cover *r* Getty Hulton; page 1 Mary Evans Picture Library; 2–3 *The Buccaneers*, by Frederick Judd Waugh (1861–1940)/Private Collection/www.bridgeman.co.uk; 4–5 Corbis/Michael S. Yamashita; 7*b* akg-images/Gilles Mermet; 8*bl* Ancient Art and Architecture Collection Ltd; 8–9*tc* akg-images/Erich Lessing; 11*br* akg-images; 12*tr* Corbis/Christie's Images; 12*bl* The Art Archive; 12–13*b* National Maritime Museum, London; 14*bl* Ancient Art & Architecture Collection Ltd; 15*tr* Mary Evans Picture Library; 14–15*b* Corbis/ Bettmann; 16*tl* Corbis/Richard T. Nowitz; 16–17 Mary Evans Picture Library; 17*tl* The Art Archive/Museo Regional de Oaxaca Mexico/Dagli Orti; 17*tr* Mary Evans Picture Library; 18*tl* akg-images/British Library; 19*t* Rex/Percy Hatchman; 20*bl* Mary Evans Picture Library; 20*tr* Heritage-Images/The British Library; 21 Mary Evans Picture Library; 22*bl* Tina Chambers © Dorling Kindersley; 23*br* Hulton Archive/Getty Images; 24*tr* Corbis/Bettmann; 24*bl* Rex/C. W. Disney/Everett (EVT); 25*b* Corbis/Bettmann; 27*tr* akg-images; 27*br* Still Pictures/Benny Odeur; 28–29*b* Mary Evans Picture Library; 29*tr* Corbis/The Mariners' Museum; 28*tr* Topfoto/British Museum/HIP; 30*bl* Corbis/Bettmann; 30*tr* akg-images/Touchstone Pictures/Album; 31*cl* akg-images; 31*r* Corbis; 32–33*b* Howard Pyle, *Marooned*, 1909, Oil on canvas, Delaware Art Museum DAM #1912-936; 32*tl* National Maritime Museum, London; 32*br* akg-images; 32*cr* Heritage-Images/The Board of Trustees of the Armouries; 33*cl* The Art Archive/Galleria Estense, Modena/Dagli Orti; 33*r* The Art Archive; 34–35 National Maritime Museum, London; 35*tr* Corbis/Asian Art & Archaeology, Inc.; 35*br* Corbis/Stapleton Collection; 36–37*b* The Art Archive/ Chateau de Blerancourt/Dagli Orti; 36*tr* Corbis/John Springer Collection; 37*br* akg-images/Arco Films/Balcazar Prod./Edic/ Rialto Films/Album; 38*bl* National Maritime Museum, London; 39*tl* Heritage-Images/The National Archives; 39*b* Topfoto; 40*tl* akg-images; 40–41*b* akg-images; 41*tr* Mary Evans Picture Library; 42*tl* Alamy/Doug Steley; 43*t* Corbis/Peter Turnley; 44*tr* Mary Evans Picture Library; 44*bl* Corbis/Bettmann; 45*tr* Corbis/Bettmann; 45*b* Corbis; 46*tl* Topfoto/PA; 47 Topfoto/PA; 48*tr* Corbis/Martin Harvey; 48*bl* Corbis/Robert Maass; 49*tr* Topfoto/Imageworks; 49*br* Corbis/Kevin Schafer; 50*b* Corbis Sygma/Fort Lauderdale Sen; 50*cr* Rex/Sipa Press (SIPA); 51 Corbis/Reuters; 52*cl* Corbis/Albrecht G. Schaefer; 52–53*c* Moreau Jean-Luc/Gamma/Katz; 53*tr* Corbis/Ricardo Azoury; 54*bl* Alamy/3C Stock; 54*tr* Topfoto/Imageworks; 55*tr* Alamy/ Iain Davidson Photographic; 55*br* Rex/Lewis Durham; 56*t* Topfoto/Public Records Office/HIP; 56*b* Corbis/Jeffrey L. Rotman; 56–57 (background) Topfoto/Public Records Office/HIP; 57*r* Alamy/Fabrice Bettex; 57*bl* Corbis/Richard T. Nowitz; 58*tl* Getty Images/Time Life Pictures; 58*tr* Corbis/Ralph White; 58*bl* Heritage Images/The British Museum; 59*cr* Corbis/Rob Howard; 60*l* akg-images/Cutthroat Productions/David James/Album; 61*r* akg-images/Cutthroat Productions/David James/Album; 62–63 (background) Ancient Art & Architecture Collection Ltd; 64*b* Mary Evans Picture Library

The publisher would like to thank the following illustrators:
Steve Weston (Linden Artists) 8–9*b*, 10–11, 26*tl*, 26–27; Encompass Graphics 22–23, 25*tr*, 46*b*

The publisher would also like to thank Ian Harvey for research assistance

Blackbeard's pirate crew